MW01069520

Dessert Designer

CRAFTING COOL CANDY CREATIONS

EYE CANDY

by Dana Meachen Rau

CAPSTONE PRESS
a capstone imprint

Snap Books are published by Capstone Press,
1710 Roe Crest Drive, North Mankato, Minnesota 56003.
www.capstonepub.com

Library of Congress Cataloging-in-Publication Data
Rau, Dana Meachen, 1971–
Eye candy : crafting cool candy creations / by Dana Meachen Rau.
p. cm.—(Snap books. Dessert designer)
Includes bibliographical references and index.
Summary: "Step-by-step instructions teach readers how to create
food art with candies"—Provided by publisher.
ISBN 978-1-4296-8620-4 (library binding)
ISBN 978-1-62065-343-2 (ebook pdf)
1. Sugar art-—Juvenile literature. 2. Candy—Juvenile literature. 3.
Confectionery—Juvenile literature. I. Title.
TX792.R38 2013
641.85'3—dc23   2012001752

Editor: Jennifer Besel
Designer: Juliette Peters
Food and Photo Stylist: Brent Bentrott
Prop Preparation: Sarah Schuette
Scheduler: Marcy Morin
Production Specialist: Kathy McColley

Photo Credits:
All photos by Capstone Studio/Karon Dubke
except:
Tania McNaboe, p. 32 (author's photo)

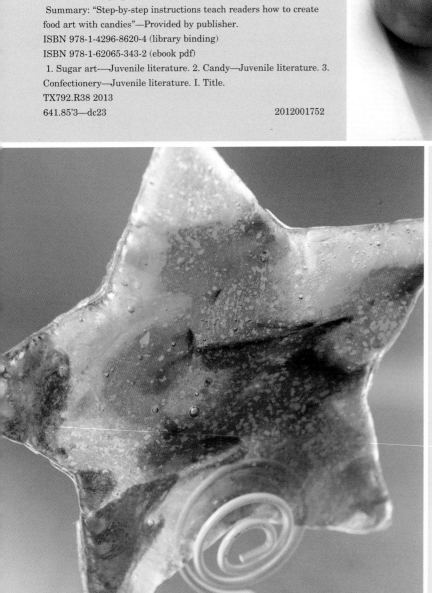

Printed in the United States of America in
North Mankato, Minnesota.
042012   006682CGF12

Table of Contents

Introduction

Extras

PLAY with YOUR FOOD

Candy is a sweet treat to eat. But who said candy was just for eating? Treat candy like craft supplies, and you'll be amazed at what you can make.

Play with candy to make the projects in this book, or make your own unique creations. And once you're done admiring your sugar sensations, cleanup is fun too. Just eat them up!

How to Use This Book

Each project lists the candies you need. Raid your cabinets to see if you have candy hidden away from a holiday or party. What you don't have, you can find at your local grocery or convenience store.

Once you have everything you need, just follow the steps to make each project. Remember, if you need to use a stove, microwave, knife, or other appliance, be sure to ask an adult for help.

DECORATOR'S TOOLBOX

A painter needs brushes and canvases. A carpenter needs hammers and nails. A candy sculptor like you needs tools too!

~ lollipop sticks ~
You'll be surprised what amazing things you can stick to the ends of these!

~ cookie sheet~
This works as well in the refrigerator as it does in the oven to keep your treats from rolling around.

~ toothpicks and wooden skewers ~
These are great for all kinds of things, including making holes in candy beads or drawing on taffy.

~ cookie cutter~
Use a cookie cutter to cut out shapes from all kinds of treats, including melted candy.

~ kitchen shears ~
These scissors are designed for use with food.

~ zip-top bags ~
Put candy in these handy bags before you crush it. They'll help keep things tidy.

~ twisty ties~
Use these handy wires to tie up goody bags.

~ wax paper ~
Use this supply to keep taffy and other sticky stuff from sticking to your workspace.

~ iron ~
It's surprising, but an iron can be a handy kitchen tool. Use it to melt licorice pieces together.

~ cooling rack ~
This tool is made to cool your goodies evenly.

~ spoons ~
Have a bunch of spoons ready to stir up your candy.

~ sharp knife ~
You need this to score or slice candy.

~ hammer ~
This tool isn't just for the wood shop! Use a hammer to crush hard candies into meltable pieces.

~ aluminum foil ~
Sure, foil keeps foods from sticking. But it also looks great as wrapping for lollipops!

~ cutting board ~
Do any cutting on the cutting board to avoid damaging kitchen counters.

~ parchment paper ~
Use this paper to line cookie sheets that will go in the oven. Unlike wax paper, parchment paper won't smoke if it gets hot.

ROLLED UP ROSES

Share the love with these edible flowers. Roses have never been this beautiful ... or sweet!

INGREDIENTS
6 packs of red fruit leather
1 pack green fruit leather

SPECIAL SUPPLIES
12 lollipop sticks

1. Cut the fruit leather into ¾-inch (2-centimeter) wide strips.

2. Cut 1-inch (2.5-cm) wide ovals from the strips. Each oval should have one straight edge. You'll need 16 "petals" for each rose.

3. Hold a lollipop stick in one hand. Roll one of the petals tightly around the top. Squeeze to mold the petal onto the stick.

4. Add the next petal, slightly overlapping the first. Squeeze the base with your fingers. Repeat with the remaining petals, moving around the flower as you go. Fold some of the petals out slightly at the top.

5. Cut two leaf shapes out of the green fruit leather. Place the wide edge of one leaf about 1 inch (2.5 cm) down from the base of your flower. Squeeze it onto the stick up to the flower's base. Repeat on the opposite side with the other leaf.

6. Repeat the steps to make additional flowers.

Makes 12 roses

Tip:
If you'd like to give these as a gift, gather them together like a bouquet. Then tie a ribbon around the middle. Wrap the bunch in a cone of paper, just like they do at a flower shop.

WINTER ICICLES

Long sparkling icicles are like winter jewelry on buildings. Bring that bling indoors, and make your home a winter wonderland.

INGREDIENTS
10 white rock candy strings
10 light blue rock candy strings
10 dark blue rock candy strings

SPECIAL SUPPLIES
16-gauge turquoise
    aluminum wire
⅛-inch (.3-cm) wide
    blue ribbon
7½-inch (19-cm) wire wreath
    frame, spray painted silver

1. Cut the aluminum wire into 30 1½-inch (4-cm) long pieces.

2. Bend both ends of each wire piece around a pencil to form hook shapes.

3. Cut four pieces of ribbon 18 inches (46 cm) long. Tie these pieces to the wire wreath, evenly spaced around the circle. Tie the loose ends together in a tight knot.

4. Wrap additional ribbon around the wire wreath to add a decorative touch.

5. Hang the wreath where you want to display it.

6. Hang the wire hooks around the wreath on the outermost ring.

7. Hang one candy string on each wire hook, alternating colors as you go around the circle.

~ Finding the Fun ~
Some stores carry rock candy strings. But in some places, they might be hard to find. If you have trouble finding them, ask a parent to order the candy strings from online stores.

RISING STARS

Let your creativity twinkle with this star-studded project. Who knew hard candy could shine so brightly?

INGREDIENTS
10 hard fruit candies

SPECIAL SUPPLIES
hammer
star-shaped cookie cutter
clear thread (optional)

Tips:
Many types of hard candies will work for this project. But only use one kind at a time. The candies may have different melting points, so mixing them could cause problems for your project.

Some ovens run a bit hotter than others. Watch your candy through the oven window. You want the candies to melt completely. But don't let them heat up so much they bubble.

1. Preheat the oven to 350 degrees Fahrenheit (177 degrees Celsius).

2. Unwrap the candies and place in a sturdy zip-top bag. With a hammer, crush the candies into powdery bits. The finer the bits, the easier they will melt.

3. Line a cookie sheet with parchment paper. Pour the crushed candies onto the paper. Gently shake the tray so the crushed candies make a flat layer. Make sure you can't see the parchment paper between any of the candy bits.

4. Place the cookie sheet in the oven for three minutes.

5. Using an oven mitt, take the tray out of the oven. Let the candy cool for two minutes.

6. Working quickly, press the cookie cutter into the melted candy. Repeat until you've made as many stars as you can.

7. If you want to hang the stars later, grab a toothpick. Poke a hole in one point of each star.

8. Carefully move the parchment from the cookie sheet to a cooling rack. Let the pieces cool and harden completely.

9. Gently lift the hardened candy from the paper. Carefully break off the candy around each star.

10. If you want to make more stars, collect the scrap pieces, recrush them, and repeat steps 1–9.

11. To hang your stars, poke a piece of clear thread through the hole in each star and tie a knot.

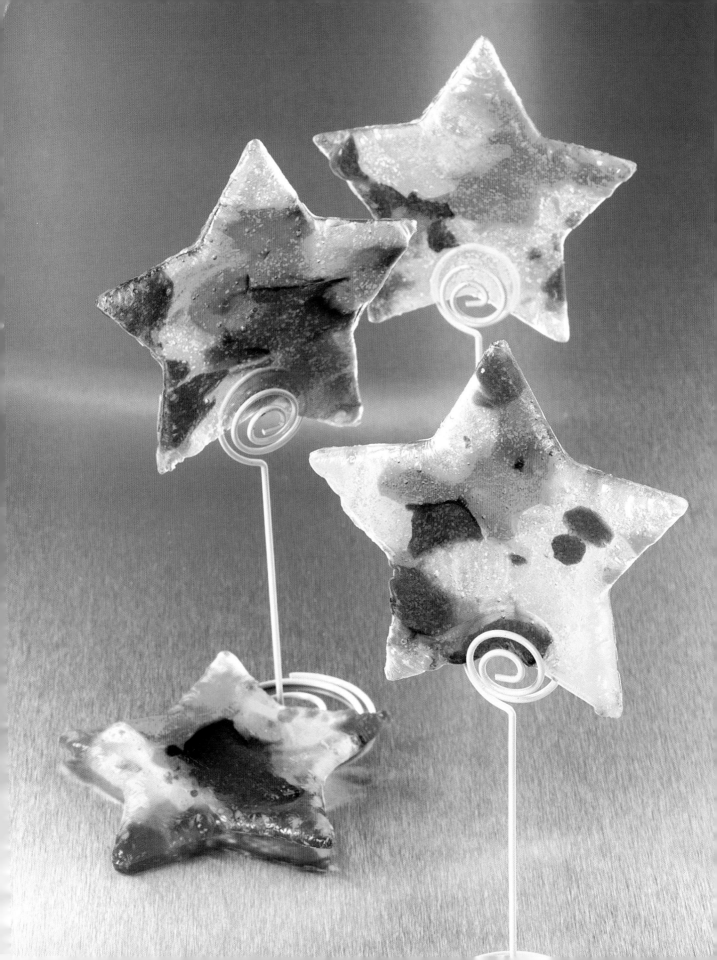

PICK·A·FLOWER PARTY FAVORS

Imagine a world where candy grows on trees. Then make it happen! Make a tree of sweet little blossom bundles that make perfect "goody bags" for your next party.

INGREDIENTS
600 small round candies

SPECIAL SUPPLIES
floral foam
small flower pot
silk flower stem
½-inch (1-cm) wide green
    grosgrain ribbon
12 9-inch (23-cm) white
    tulle circles
12 green twisty ties

1. With a knife, cut the piece of floral foam to fit into the flower pot. Poke the end of the stem into the foam.

2. Cut 12 pieces of ribbon 6 inches (15 cm) long.

3. Separate the candies by color.

4. Place 50 candies of the same or similar colors in the center of a tulle circle. Gather up the sides and twist. Tie a piece of ribbon tightly around the tulle to hold in the candies.

5. Repeat step 4 with the other tulle pieces and candies.

6. Attach each blossom to the flower stem with a green twisty tie.

> *Tip:*
> Instead of buying a fake stem for this project, you could use a real branch. If you use a real branch, try to find one that is clean and sturdy. A branch that has lots of extra little branches works nicely.

LICORICE TWIST BUTTERFLIES

Bug out your family and friends. This unusual use of licorice will have them fluttering with excitement.

INGREDIENTS
rainbow licorice twists

SPECIAL SUPPLIES
iron

1. Turn a cookie sheet upside down on your workspace. Cover it with a dish towel. Place a piece of parchment paper on top of the towel.

2. On a cutting board, cut the licorice twists into ¼-inch (.6-cm) slices with a knife to form star-shaped beads. You need two blue, six green, 14 purple, 16 red, and 18 yellow beads to make the butterfly. Or use whatever colors you want!

3. Arrange the beads on the piece of parchment in the shape of a butterfly. Start with a center line as its body. Then place the beads symmetrically on each side. Make sure the beads are all touching.

4. Put another piece of parchment paper on top of your butterfly. With a dry iron set on the cotton setting, press the iron down on the parchment. Hold it in place for 10 to 15 seconds. Lift the iron and set aside.

5. Carefully flip over the pieces of parchment with the butterfly inside. Press the iron on the other side of the parchment for 10 to 15 seconds.

6. Peel off the top piece of parchment. Let the bead butterfly cool completely.

~ Endless Possibilities ~
You can make any shape you want with this project. Just make sure every licorice bead touches at least one other bead before ironing. Then your project will be nice and sturdy.

CANDY SHAKE

Layer up the candy for this twist on a milkshake. This treat is so sweet, friends will want to take it home to eat. And they don't have to worry about it melting!

INGREDIENTS
pink, white, and brown candies
   (Use any kinds you like!)
cotton candy
candy cane stick
1 red candy

1. In a clear glass, make a layer of pink candy.

2. Place a layer of white candy on top of the pink.

3. Sprinkle in some brown candies to look like hot fudge.

4. Make a small layer of white candy. Then add a small layer of pink.

5. Next add a layer of brown candies.

6. Place a bit of cotton candy on top to look like whipped cream.

7. Stick the candy cane into the candy shake. Then put a red candy on top like a cherry.

Tip:
These candy shakes make fun party place cards. Layer the candy in clear plastic cups. Write your guests' names on the outside of each cup with a permanent marker. Place one shake at each spot so they know where to sit. Then they can nibble on the treats for dessert.

mix·and·match MONSTERS

Show off your scary side with these gummy monsters. With just a few candy details, create a whole crew of creatures with attitude.

INGREDIENTS
large sugared gumdrops
vanilla frosting

For the monster's features, use any small candies you like. Here are some ideas:

banana-shaped candies
candy buttons
licorice whips
rainbow licorice twists
rainbow sprinkles
round breath mints
round gummy candies
small breath mints
small gumdrops
sugar pearls
wafer candies

1. Use large gumdrops as the monsters' bodies. Use a toothpick to dig small holes in the gumdrops. Put holes wherever you want to add facial features.

2. Use different candies to make faces for your monsters. Put the candies into the holes you dug to make them stick.

3. Add hair, feet, or other features to your monsters. Use dabs of vanilla frosting to stick on large candies.

Be creative and have fun!

sweet sushi

Try this twist on sushi. And fool your family with dinner for dessert!

INGREDIENTS

1 large marshmallow
1 red and 1 green gumdrop
1 crispy rice marshmallow treat
2 packs green fruit leather
8 round cinnamon candies
1 piece each of pink, orange, and white taffy

1. Cut the marshmallow in half width wise with the kitchen shears. The cut ends will be sticky.

2. With a knife, cut off the round tops from both gumdrops. Then cut the tops in half lengthwise. Press one red piece and one green piece together. Repeat with the other red and green pieces

3. Cut off about ½ inch (1 cm) from one end of the crispy rice treat. Mold the cut piece in a circle around a red/green gumdrop. Make the circle the same size as the marshmallow half from step 1. Then place the crispy circle on the sticky end of one marshmallow half.

4. With the kitchen shears, cut a strip of fruit leather the same height as the marshmallow and crispy circle. Roll the fruit leather strip around the marshmallow and crispy circle. Press the end to seal.

5. Repeat steps 3 and 4. Then stick eight cinnamon candies on top of this piece to look like fish eggs.

6. Warm the pink, orange, and white taffy in the microwave for about five seconds. Place each one between two pieces of wax paper, and roll them flat with a rolling pin.

7. Mold the pink taffy into a long rectangle. Use a toothpick to draw evenly spaced lines across the top of the taffy to look like tuna.

8. Mold the orange taffy into a long rectangle. Then trim one end to look like a tail. Use a toothpick to draw lines on the top of this "shrimp."

9. With kitchen shears, cut thin strips out of the white taffy. Lay two strips across the pink taffy. Lay two strips slightly curved across the orange taffy. Press the strips down gently to lay flat.

10. With a knife, cut two 2-inch (5-cm) rectangles from the crispy rice treat. Place the tuna on one piece and the shrimp on the other.

11. Cut two thin strips of fruit leather. Wrap them around the tuna and shrimp and crispy rice rectangles.

EARTH BEAD BRACELET

Home sweet home. Celebrate our home planet with an Earth-inspired bracelet. Made with "candy clay," it shows off our sweet home indeed!

INGREDIENTS

2.5 ounces (71 grams) each of green and blue candy melting wafers

8 teaspoons (40 mL) light corn syrup

SPECIAL SUPPLIES

2–3 wooden skewers

3 12-inch (30-cm) long blue or green hemp beading cords

1. Place the green melting wafers in a microwave safe bowl and heat according to the package directions. When the wafers are fully melted, add 4 teaspoons of light corn syrup. Stir until smooth dough forms.

2. Place the dough on a piece of wax paper. Flatten with a spoon slightly so it is about ¼-inch (.6-cm) thick.

3. Repeat steps 1 and 2 with the blue melting wafers.

4. Set the doughs aside for 30 minutes to harden. They will become stiff like clay.

5. Pinch off a piece of blue dough and roll it into a ½-inch (1-cm) ball. Then pinch off three to five smaller pieces of green dough and stick them onto the blue ball. Roll the ball again so that all the dough is flat and smooth.

6. Repeat with the rest of the dough, rolling beads of blue and sticking on small pieces of green.

7. With a toothpick, poke a hole through each dough bead. Run the toothpick back and forth through the beads so that they can move freely. Reroll the beads gently if they get a little stretched when you push the toothpick through.

8. Thread the beads onto skewers, leaving a small space between each bead. Put the skewers on a cookie sheet.

9. Place the cookie sheet in the refrigerator for an hour. Check on the beads every 15 minutes to make sure they roll freely and aren't sticking to the skewer or to each other.

10. Remove the beads from the skewers.

11. Hold the beading cords together evenly across your workspace. Thread 12 beads onto the cords. Hold the bracelet around your wrist to check the size. Add or remove beads for the perfect fit.

12. Tie both ends of the beading cord together to secure.

FLOWER TURTLES

After a busy day, a turtle treat might help slow things down. But prepare yourself. These tasty turtles will move fast when friends get a taste!

INGREDIENTS
12 pieces sliced almonds
60 pieces slivered almonds
12 chocolate-covered caramels
1 sheet candy buttons

1. Preheat the oven to 350 degrees Fahrenheit (177 degrees Celsius).

2. Line a cookie sheet with parchment paper.

3. Place a sliced almond on the paper as the head. Place five slivered almonds in a star shape to make the legs and tail. Make sure the legs and tail all meet in a center point.

4. Place a chocolate-covered caramel on the center point of the almond star.

5. Repeat steps 3–4 with the rest of the almonds and chocolate-covered caramels.

6. Bake the turtles for about three to four minutes, enough to start melting the chocolate and caramel.

7. With an oven mitt, take the cookie sheet out of the oven. While the chocolate is still warm, place the candy buttons on top of the "shells" in a flower shape. Push the candy down gently. The chocolate will spread out a little.

8. When the cookie sheet is cool to the touch, place it in the refrigerator so the turtles can harden.

Tip:
You don't have to use almonds for this project. Look for other nuts or nut pieces shaped like heads, legs, and tails. Peanuts or cashews would work well too.

LOLLIPOP DISCO BALL

Get the party started with this glittery disco ball. But this decoration won't go to waste. It'll provide sweet treats for your guests when the dancing is done.

INGREDIENTS
250 to 300 small
round lollipops

SPECIAL SUPPLIES
1 7-inch (18-cm) Styrofoam
ball
plastic beaded necklace
250 to 300 4-inch (10-cm)
squares of aluminum foil

~ Light It Up ~
You can make this disco ball into a light for your dance floor. Before you push in the lollipops, wrap the ball with a string of white lights. Tape the lights down in a few places. Then push in the pops to cover the cords, letting the lights stick out between them. The lights will reflect off the foil and really make your disco ball shine!

1. With a long wooden skewer, poke a hole through the center of the ball from top to bottom. Thread the plastic necklace through the hole. Use the wooden skewer to help push the necklace through.

2. Tie one end of the necklace in a knot. Make sure the knot is much bigger than the hole. The disco ball will get heavy, and you need to be sure the necklace won't slip out. Pull the necklace so the knot is even with the bottom of the disco ball and you have a loop for hanging at the top.

3. Place the top of a lollipop in the center of an aluminum foil square. Gather the corners of the foil around the base of the lollipop and twist to tighten the paper. Repeat on all of the lollipops.

4. Poke the lollipops into the ball in a horizontal line around the middle. Space the lollipops about 1 inch (2.5 cm) apart.

5. Add a second line just above the first, tucking each lollipop between the ones on the first line.

6. Continue adding lines of pops all the way up to the top.

7. Repeat on the lower half of the ball, adding rings of lollipops until you reach the knot on the bottom.

INGREDIENTS GLOSSARY

fruit leather

rock candy strings

hard fruit candy

rainbow licorice twists

licorice whips

cotton candy

large sugared gumdrops

sugar pearls

round breath mints

round gummy candies

small gumdrops

candy buttons

banana-shaped candies

small breath mints

candy cane stick

rainbow sprinkles

wafer candies

round cinnamon candies

crispy rice marshmallow treats

small round lollipops

taffy

chocolate-covered caramels

sliced almonds

slivered almonds

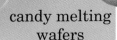

candy melting wafers

Read more

Bowers, Sharon. *Candy Construction: How to Build Edible Race Cars, Castles, and Other Cool Stuff Out of Store-Bought Candy!* North Adams, Mass.: Storey Pub., 2010.

Candy Bouquets: Create Your Own Gifts & Centerpieces. Delicious Designs. Waverly, Iowa: CQ Products, 2008.

Dunnington, Rose. *Sweet Eats: Mmmore Than Just Desserts.* New York: Lark Books, 2008.

Internet sites

FactHound offers a safe, fun way to find Internet sites related to this book. All of the sites on FactHound have been researched by our staff.

Here's all you do:
Visit *www.facthound.com*
Type in this code: 9781429686204

About the Author

Dana Meachen Rau writes about many topics, including food! When she's not writing, she's being creative in other ways—especially in the kitchen. Sometimes she follows recipes, but other times she experiments with new flavors. And she doesn't need a special occasion to whip up a special dessert for her friends and family in Burlington, Connecticut.

 Super-cool stuff! Check out projects, games and lots more at **www.capstonekids.com**